Great Minds
colouring book

Renaissance Press
http://renaissancebookpress.com
info@renaissancebookpress.com

Renaissance

Diverse Canadian Voices

Great Minds
colouring book

pioneers of science
you may have never heard of

Nathan Caro
Fréchette

Srinivasa Ramanujan
1887 - 1920

Srinivasa Ramanujan was an Indian mathematician with almost no formal training. He made great contributions to number theory, infinite series, and mathematical analysis. He also solved a few mathematical problems thought to be unsolvable.

Ramanujan compiled nearly 4,000 results, some so groundbreaking they took decades to prove, but his calculations have now nearly all been proven correct.

He was the first Indian to be elected a Fellow of Trinity College, Cambridge.

"I have not trodden through a conventional university course, but I am striking out a new path for myself. ."
- Srinivasa Ramanujan

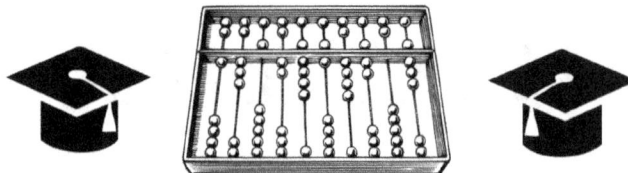

Vera Rubin
1928 - 2016

Vera Rubin was an astronomer. She pioneered work on galaxy rotation rates, discovering a discrepancy between the predicted angular motion of galaxies and what was observed. Her "galaxy rotation problem" eventually became recognized as evidence of the existence of dark matter.

Rubin spent a lot of her life advocating for women in science, and mentored aspiring women astronomers.

"Science progresses best when observations force us to alter our preconceptions."
- Vera Rubin

Florence Nightingale
1820 - 1910

Florence Nightingale was an English statistician who helped popularize the graphical presentation of data. She is also responsible for a large reform in hospital hygiene practices.

Nightingale is most widely known for founding the modern profession of nursing. The establishment of her nursing school provided opportunities for women, and legitimized work outside the home.

"Were there none who were discontented with what they have,
the world would never reach anything better."
- Florence Nightingale

Percy Lavon Julian
1899 - 1975

Percy Lavon Julian was a chemist and a pioneer in research on the synthesis of human hormones from plants, notably progesterone and testosterone. His research contributed to modern birth control and hormone replacement therapy.

He was the first Black chemist inducted into the National Academy of Science.

"I don't think that you can possibly embrace the kind of joy
which one who has worked with plants and plant structures
such as I have over a period of nearly 40 years,
how wonderful the plant laboratory seems."
- Percy Lavon Julian

George Washington Carver
1860s - 1943

George Washington Carver was born into slavery, but pursued an education after slavery was abolished, earning a bachelor's degree in agricultural science.

He encouraged farmers to adopt sustainable practices, developed more than 300 industrial uses for alternative crops like peanuts and sweet potatoes, and was a leader in the promotion of environmentalism.

"Education is key to unlock the golden door of freedom."
- George Washington Carver

Sofia Kovalevskaya
1850 - 1891

Sofia Kovalevskaya was a mathematician who made significant contributions to analysis, mecanics, and partial diferential equations.

She was the first woman to be appointed to a full professorship in Northern Europe.

"It seems to me that the poet has only to perceive that which others do not perceive, to look deeper than others look. And the mathematician must do the same thing."
— Sofia Kovalevskaya

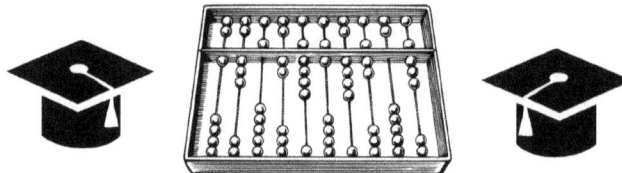

Hedy Lamarr
1914 - 2000

Hedy Lamarr was a self-taught inventor, and in WWII, developed a radio guidance system for Allied torpedoes; the principles of this system are now used for modern WiFi and Bluetooth technology.

She was also a Hollywood actress, and starred in a few blockbuster movies such as *Samson and Delilah*.

"All creative people want to do the unexpected."
- Hedy Lamarr

Rosalind Franklin
1920 - 1958

Rosalind Franklin was a chemist and an X-ray crystallographer. Her work concentrated on the molecular structure of viruses, coal and graphite.

Her research played a pivotal role to the discovery of the structure of DNA and RNA.

"Science and everyday life cannot and should not be separated."
- Rosalind Franklin

Grace Hopper
1906 - 1992

Grace Hopper was a computer scientist and a U.S. Navy rear admiral. She pioneered the idea that programming languages should be machine-independent, and invented a compiler which could compile an English-based computer language into machine code. This led to the creation of the first programing languages, including COBOL.

She was awarded 40 honorary degrees from universities across the world, and the National Medal of Technilogy.

"A ship in port is safe, but that's not what ships are built for."
- Grace Hopper

Mary Maynard Dayly
1921 - 2003

Mary Maynard Daly was a biochemist, and the first Black woman in the US to earn a Ph.D. in chemistry. She conducted important studies on cholesterol, sugars, and protein. Her research contributed to better understanding heart and lung disease.

In addition to her research, she was also very dedicated to programs to increase the enrollment of minority students in graduate science programs.

"I'm a complete deviant. All creative work breaks new ground."
- Mary Maynard Daly

Magnus Hirschfeld
1868 - 1935

Magnus Hirschfeld was a Jewish German physician who pioneered the field of sexology and sexual research. He was the first to research homosexuality and transgender people not out of a desire to cure them of it, but because he believed that a better scientific understanding of sexual minorities would eliminate social hostility toward them. A lot of his research was unfortunately destroyed by the Nazis during WWII.

"The more we delve into the essence of personality, the more we learn that in this world, certainly rich with natural beauty and things worthy of seeing, nothing is more attractive and worthier of knowing and experiencing than people."

\- Magnus Hirschfeld

Mary Leaky
1913 - 1996

Mary Leaky was a paleoanthropologist who specialized in hominin fossils. She discovered the many famous fossils, including the first Proconsul skull, the Laetoli footprints, fifteen new species of animals, and hominin fossils that were over 3.75 milion years old.

"Theories come and go, but fundamental data
always remains the same."
- Mary Leaky

Katherine Johnson
1918 -

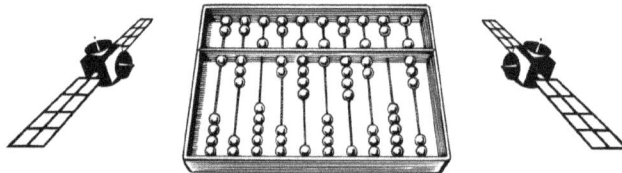

Katherine Johnson is a brilliant mathematician who spent most of her career working for NASA. She was responsible for a lot of the math involved in several space launches, doing trajectory analysis for America's first human spaceflight.

Most famously, in 1962, NASA was preparing to send up the Friendship 7's mission, they used computers to calculate the trajectory. The astronaut John Glenn asked that Katherine Johnson check all the computer's calculations by hand, and only after she had said everything was correct would he board the flight.

"Everything is physics and math."
- Katherine Johnson

Inge Lehmann
1888 - 1993

Inge Lehmann was a seismologist and geophysicist. For years, scientists had been unable to explain the measurements of seismic waves from earthquakes, which didn't fit the pattern predicted with the accepted model of the Earth at the time.

It was Lehmann's careful analysis of these waves which led to her discovery that the Earth's core was solid, and not molten as had ben previously believed.

"You should know how many incompetent men
I had to compete with - in vain."
- Inge Lehmann

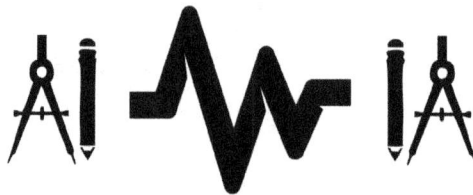

Marie Curie
1867 - 1934

Marie Curie was a physicist who pioneered research on radioactivity, so much so that she actually coined the term "radioactivity". She discovered several elements, including radium and polonium, and her research was instrumental in cancer treatment.

She was the first woman to win a Nobel Prize and the first person to win it in two disciplines. She never patented the medical applications of radium, so that it could be widely available to heal.

"Nothing in life is to be feared; it is only to be understood."
- Marie Curie

Chien-Shiung Wu
1912 - 1998

Chen-Shiung Wu was an Chinese-American experimental physicist. Her research on particles won her colleagues the 1957 Nobel prize, though her work was not acknowledged.

Wu was the first woman to become president of the American Physical Society, received the first honorary doctorate awarded to a woman by Princeton University, and her book *Beta Decay* is stil a standard reference for nuclear physicists.

"There is only one thing worse than coming home from the lab to a sink full of dirty dishes, and that is not going to the lab at all!"
- Chien-Shiung Wu

Ada Lovelace
1815 - 1852

Ada Lovelace was a mathematician and writer, who was the first to recognize full potential the aplications of Charles Babbage's Analytical Engine beyond just a mechanical calculator, and is largely acknowledged as the world's first computer programmer.

"We may say most aptly that the Analytical Engine weaves algebraical patterns just as the Jacquard loom weaves flowers and leaves."
- Ada Lovelace

Annie Jump Cannon
1863 - 1941

Annie Jump Cannon was a Deaf astronomer and suffragette. Her contributions to our understanding of the stars are nearly immesurable. Her exhaustive work classifying the stars by their spectral types led to the understanding of their temperature and composition. She personally classified over 350,000 stars, and was the first woman to obtain an honorary Doctorate of Science from Oxford, in 1925.

Her star classification system was adopted by the International Astronomical Union in 1922, and it remains in use to this day.

"Classifying the stars has helped materially in all studies of the structure of the universe."

- Annie Jump Cannon

Clair Patterson
1922 - 1995

Clair Patterson was a geochemist whose first important breakthrough was calculating the age of the Earth, using the lead-lead dating method he had developed from the uranium-lead dating method.

This led him quickly to a second important discovery: the lead contained in gasoline was contaminating everything, leading to dangerously high lead levels in cities which were beginning to poison some people.

He spent most of his life fighting the oil companies to get them to remove the lead from their product.

"True scientific discovery renders the brain incapable at such moments of shouting vigorously to the world "Look at what I've done! Now I will reap the benefits of recognition and wealth." Instead such discovery instinctively forces the brain to thunder "We did it" in a voice no one else can hear, within its sacred, but lonely, chapel of scientific thought."
- Clair Patterson

Michael Faraday
1791 - 1867

Michael Faraday came from a humble background with little formal education, but his contributions to science are some of the most significant in history.

Faraday was the first to understand how magnetism and electricity worked, how they interacted, and how they could be harnessed and used. He invented the very first electric motor, and his work is responsible for our modern use or electricity in technology.

He was also a chemist, who discovered benzene and invented an early version of the Bunsen burner.

"No matter what you look at, if you look at it closely enough, you are involved in the entire universe."
- Michael Faraday

Sir Chandrasekhara Venkata Raman
1888 - 1970

Sir Chandrasekhara Vankata Raman was an Indian physicist. His work on light scattering won him the Nobel Prize for Physics in 1930, for discovering the 'Raman effect'.

"Ask the right questions, and nature will open
the doors to her secrets."
- Sir Chandrasekhara Venkata Raman

www.ingramcontent.com/pod-product-compliance
Lightning Source LLC
LaVergne TN
LVHW080249090426
835508LV00042BA/1500